Praise for *Whitewash*

"Frances Victory Schenkkan's *Whitewash* confronts its complex shames and complicated confessions with an imaginative resolve. The power of documentary poetics makes these poems sing a new liturgy for old Louisiana, for the poet's own Shreveport, and for a history that's difficult to face. Poem after poem turns toward various personas caught in the rationalization of complicity, the beauty of landscape, and the mythos each family makes. To say Schenkkan's stellar poems reckon with history isn't enough, because every line seeks to 'burst out, into the grievous streets.'"

—Steven Leyva, author of *The Opposite of Cruelty*

"One of the heaviest lessons I've learned being born, raised, and living in Louisiana my whole life is just how much we all bear the weight of our collective past—all the injustices, poor decisions, and misheld traditions we carry into today. Our statues, our street names, our prom pictures taken in front of crumbling plantations—there are living reminders everywhere. Seeing it all for exactly what it is, then and now, is the first important step toward a better tomorrow here. Frances Victory Schenkkan's new collection, *Whitewash*, helps us do exactly that by shining the clearest of lights on the history we share, the memories we hold dear, and this place we call home. Line by line, Schenkkan offers family histories, cultural memories, and hard truths we need to move forward. And while these poems cannot right wrongs, nor can they repay debts, they do their absolute best to deliver the gifts only honesty and clarity can give. For those gifts, I am tremendously grateful."

—Jack B. Bedell, author of *Ghost Forest*,
Poet Laureate of Louisiana, 2017–2019

"*Whitewash* navigates the multidimensional tensions between poverty, place, and race. In Schenkkan's rich and reaching poems, we are made to confront the intricate and even convoluted realities of racism and complicity without escape and without the possibility of transcendence save for the abundant voice and lyricism pressed upon a physical and psychological landscape and narrative history. These poems offer an opportunity to participate in a social context that can (re)shape what we think of now as historical experience even

as we relive so much of this book's emotional tension and tenor today. This is an ambitious collection. Impeccably researched and passionately nuanced, these are poems that demand we contemplate all that frames how we memorialize the past's erased sins and troubled beauty that weighs upon us all."

—Joshua Robbins, author of *Eschatology in Crayon Wax*

Praise for *Mr. Stevens' Secretary*

"Frances Schenkkan's poems provide a fresh perspective on the brilliant, enigmatic Wallace Stevens, whose inimitable music still haunts us sixty years after his death. . . . By giving us Stevens' fictive secretary . . . trying all the while to comprehend the elusive giant, Schenkkan manages as only a poet can to reveal a great deal about who this solitary genius was."

—Paul Mariani

"As we get to know [Stevens' secretary as Schenkkan imagines her] in these fiercely intelligent poems . . . we finish richer for her inspired lyrics."

—April Ossmann

"Like Carol Ann Duffy's boldly feminist collection, *The World's Wife*, Frances Schenkkan's *Mr. Stevens' Secretary* forces readers to adjust their perspective by showing a great man through the eyes of a previously silent and less visible woman."

—Billy Collins

WHITEWASH

WHITEWASH

Frances Victory Schenkkan

poems

Fort Smith, Arkansas

Whitewash

Cover image: Photo by Russell Lee, 1941
(Farm Security Administration/Office of War Information
Black-and-White Collection)

Author photo: Cristina Speligene Umezawa

Edited by Casie Dodd
Design & typography by Belle Point Press

Belle Point Press, LLC
Fort Smith, Arkansas
bellepointpress.com
editor@bellepointpress.com

Find Belle Point Press
on Facebook, Substack,
and Instagram (@bellepointpress)

28 27 26 25 24 1 2 3 4 5

Library of Congress Control Number: 2024945500

ISBN: 978-1-960215-25-3

WHW/BPP37

To the citizens of my hometown—Shreveport—
who see its flaws, and potential

I

II

Be sloop in motion,
wayward boat, mind afloat

then off again
to the homely Red River
always a stop there

Lou-is-i-ana! Lou-is-i-ana!
that dear old state of ours

Resolve

—in a letter to a friend

"If Earlene keeps up with the ironing,
if Lallie isn't sick or Frank Jr.,
if Elizabeth Grace would do it, too,
if I could spare the five dollars
and my mother-in-law doesn't say no
and Frank says it's okay with him
being it was Pastor who told us both
this Southern Women Against Lynching
is doing the Lord's work, I'd join."

Who Speaks Here

A woman my mother might have known
resolves—or does she?—to support
an anti-lynching group. Whether to go
to the funeral of her maid's son.

A girl I might have known describes
a Black mother and her daughter
on the trolley, the mother taken by police.
A teen writes in her diary:

she's invited to swim in an integrated pool.
What about her father? He mustn't know.
The personas I have created here help
me look as straight as I can at Shreveport,

where I grew up. Tensions about race
were evident to anyone paying attention.
I wasn't, except for the drama, to my shame.
My family didn't talk about *rights,*

despite sit-ins at the Woolworth downtown.
A deacon whispered: *they'll force their way*
into the church; my father: *they'll riot.*
Shreveport was where he had made

something of himself—how dare Blacks
think they could do the same. Be equal.
I turned away from him.
And from my racially divided city, too.

Going Home. Who Comes With Me.

Shame offers herself right away.
She puts on her coat and hat and, look,
here comes her finger-wagging twin, Confession.

I'd rather bring Control, with her lists.
But let's start. A first memory: there's me
in the foreground, four years old, in a sun suit—

yellow straps with strawberry buttons—
and there's my brother crossing the street.
His legs were switched for leaving the yard,

plus the neighbor's dog bit him.
I was switched too, just for watching
from behind the wisteria.

Jeff was okay, but, Shame asks,
Could I have kept him in the yard?
Confession hisses, Not yet, too young.

The dog could stand for grief,
how we should welcome it in,
it's been under the porch all along.

My trip's only beginning, and already
I am talking about grief. We were children.
The dog was real, snarling, and scared us.

For Alexander, Amos, Charlotte, Dicke, Durnbonell, George, Jacob, Jennie, Sarah, and Stephen

1. *I came from people too poor to own slaves* is something I have said.

2. A list of slaves and their owners in Matagorda County, TX, a voter registration list for 1867–70, and family records from the mid-1800s show Rugeleys, the family name of my great-great-grandmother and my grandmother's middle name, owning ten slaves.

3. A "Cpt. Rugeley" owned three. My grandmother's great-grandfather, whose name was John, was a captain in the Texas Army. One of his sons, "Capn. Ned," mounted a cavalry company from his own means during the Civil War.

4. In a will written before coming to Texas in 1840, John Rugeley lists 30 slaves to be passed on to his children in the event of his or his wife's death. Some are listed in this poem's title.

5. Alexander Irwin Rugeley, John's son, inherited six slaves. County records list "Durnbonell (African)" at a plantation owned by "Dr. Rugeley."

6. In 1860, Matagorda County, where the Rugeleys lived, counted 2,144 residents plus 1,348 slaves.

7. Matagorda and nearby South Texas counties had the most slaves in the state. One in four Texas families owned slaves.

8. Between about 1810 and 1865, Matagorda Port was a major entry point for slaves brought in to pick cotton and cut sugar cane at area plantations. Some slaves were baptized at Christ Episcopal Church, which now stands at 206 Cypress Street.

9. John Rugeley advertised a $50 reward for a runaway slave in the *Matagorda Gazette* on Christmas Day, 1858.

10. Across the state line, Shreveport had a slave market. In 1860 its population was 2,200 free citizens and 1,300 slaves.

11. In the 1790s, some Baptist assemblies, including ones in Virginia and Georgia, opposed slavery.

12. I was raised as a Baptist in Shreveport. Henry Rugeley, the immigrant patriarch in America of my father's branch of the Rugeleys, was christened an Anglican at St. Ives, England. I do not know when my mother's and father's families or their ancestors became Baptist.

13. Henry Rugeley owned slaves in South Carolina. In 1791 and again in 1792 he wrote to his brother Matthew in England: "Permit me to draw upon you £200/300 to purchase some Negroes." The next letter asks for £310 to purchase six more.

Resolve

—while talking long distance

"I was watering my roses yesterday
and heard the new little girl next door
ask the maid, 'Miss Lily, may I swing
'til supper's ready?' and I don't know
where that family's from, but here
we don't call the maid 'Miss'
or 'Mrs.' either, and our Earlene
walks with 'Miss Lily' to the trolley
and she's asked, I bet, about wages,
so I might consider 'Miss Earlene'
as it does sound a bit classy
and it's better than raising her pay."

My Credentials

White diapers, white shoes, white petticoat first day of school.
A white Bible for Sunday School.
White lipstick, briefly, my first bra white,
white boyfriends. Mother made coconut cake Fridays.
White bread for breakfast, lunch, and dinner. Grits.
White sorority sisters and the French teacher, the football
coach, too, white Elvis on the radio. White editors
in every section of the first newspaper I worked for.
Two writers in the society section wore white gloves.
White dress, white slip, white shoes for my wedding, white husband.
Whites only on every block I have lived on, in every building.
My white legs, my white face will not tan.
The dermatologist, white, warns me not to keep trying.

It Wasn't Us

After the lynching, his family moved away from the South,
specifically Caddo Parish, where 48 African Americans
were hanged between 1877 and 1950.

Only two counties in the country lynched more Blacks.

Today, Thomas Miles' name is among those on giant slabs
at the National Lynching Memorial in Montgomery.
Dirt from the site of his hanging is there for all to see,

including his great-granddaughter who, in an oral history,
said she cried. She said she felt angry and frustrated.
She said she wanted to talk, to be quiet, "so many emotions."

In 1912, the year Thomas Miles was hanged, my parents
didn't live in the parish. Later, their adopted home
was among parishes fostering a White Citizens Council

to keep Blacks from voting, keep schools segregated, and
keep public transport "separate but equal." I never heard
my parents speak of it—for or against—by which I mean

I come from people who keep quiet,
who mind their own business,
who don't go to what some would call *extremes.*

The Great Raft

Port was in its name—Shreveport—
but school trips were to Coca-Cola where
bottle after green bottle filled up brown.

Were we taught how the city got its name?
Maybe I wasn't listening, my father holding forth
about the Battle of Mansfield, Mother humming

her hymns, dipping the night's tripe
into cornmeal to fry. In the living room,
gold-edged volumes of *The World Book*

lined up. I could have read how in the 1830s
workers cleared The Great Raft of fallen trees
in the Red River by using a "snag boat"

invented by "Captain" Shreve of New Jersey.
It pulled trees from the river and ground them.
My hometown got going: a thriving slave market

and commerce that we looked down on—the aunt
who worked for the railroad, an uncle in insurance—
as if farms and timber mills were not in our history.

Mother's father ran a grocery; later, her widowed
mother took in boarders. Today, God bless us,
every scrap of land we own we frack.

Gladstone Boulevard

The quiet street I grew up on
was hardly a boulevard, didn't even try
to live up to its namesake—

Prime Minister, Chancellor of the Exchequer
William Ewart Gladstone, who until late in 1862
hoped Lincoln would back off about the slaves:

divide the country if it got the cotton flowing
again to England. In Manchester, in Lancaster,
textile workers were starving. Also, his father

owned slaves, thousands, in the West Indies.
Gladstone changed his mind, though,
after Antietam. We didn't hear it from my father.

Was it chance that he, still bitter in 1926
at the South's loss, built a house on Gladstone?
My father could depend on ignorance,

starting with his daughter. Growing up,
I said *Gladstone Boulevard* with pride,
not knowing much of anything.

Mythical Childhood

Whatever I find interesting, my mother does, too.

I know how to tell jokes.

My father's garden is full of tomatoes. Mother's fried chicken is the best in town, he says.

We have a fire in the fireplace when it gets the slightest bit cold.

I am never left out when we play jacks at recess.

I know what to call all the parts of my body because Mother taught me.

Inside our house it smells like lemon.

If I don't understand something, I can just ask.

I'm not short.

Mrs. Murphy hung my drawing of a daffodil on the classroom door.

What will he come up with next? Father sometimes says after the sermon.

My oldest sister teaches me hymns on the piano and sings as I play "Abide With Me." Then we Jitterbug.

When Mother cooks a new recipe, she invites the couple next door. He whistles when he's mowing the yard. They aren't white and don't go to First Baptist.

I can catch a fly ball, or most of the time.

When I hit a home run, my brother shouts, *There she goes!*

Resolve

—after a request

"She's asked me to come to the funeral
though I've never even met her son,
how would I meet a Negro boy,
just saw him that once on the porch
when I took her home because of the rain,
and now he's come back from Italy in a box,
this damn war, the boy was only 19,
but it sure is a lot to ask
though I guess I could slip in the back and
I wouldn't stay for the lunch, of course,
and it does seem the right thing,
the Christian thing, and patriotic."

When Martin Luther King, Jr. Spoke in Shreveport, August, 1958

I was likely playing Red Rover
with the children from next door
or we were running through the pesticide
city trucks sprayed to kill mosquitoes.

Galilee Missionary Baptist Church
didn't have enough parking for 500.
Police gave tickets to any cars parked
on the street. Sand was poured

into some gas tanks. Inside, King
urged listeners to feel *agape*
for people who did such things.
Love them because God loves them,

meet physical force with soul force,
he said. But don't stop trying
to integrate buses in Shreveport,
be like those who followed Gandhi,

a little brown man, to the sea
when a tax on salt was imposed.
Be like the Israelites who kept on
when things got tough in the wilderness.

We knew about Moses, knew the commandment
you shall love your neighbor as yourself
and we tried to obey, though the neighbor
yelled at his wife. King reminded

the crowd that *No man is an island.*
On the tape, you can hear voices shouting
That's right. What you can't hear
is the smashing of windshields.

Terms of Reduction

My aunt gives tomatoes from her garden
to her friend, a Negro. She knows him from work.

I don't tell my parents and wonder why she tells me.
My aunt's confusing: father a minister—

Unitarian? Congregational?—but Sundays
instead of church she and my uncle play tennis.

They live in the attic of my grandmother's house
past the college. He fixes radios and is writing something.

He's called Son so we children call him Uncle Son.
I think anyone except my grandmother calling him

son is odd. He's not *my* son. It's like *boy*,
which I sometimes hear said to the Negro

working at the filling station. He's a grown man.
It's not like *son*, said with affection.

Resolve

—talking with a friend

"Lallie is dying to see Elvis Presley at the *Hayride.*
She knows not to ask Frank and she wants me to
say she's spending the night with Jennifer, which
she would. She just won't let up about it.
She's going around the house singing that ditty
he did for Southern Maid about how donuts
hit the spot and you can get them piping hot.
What? The *Hayride* wouldn't have a Negro.
I don't see the harm in letting her go this once.
My mother-in-law would roll over in her grave."

Girl Reporter, 1959

The girl's about my age, eight,
and I'm already seated when they get on.
I'm holding my Bible, for Sunday School,

and start unzipping it. Then zip it.
Unzip. I'm by myself only because
Mother's in the hospital. I can't visit.

It's *something female,* my aunt said.
Father's coming to church, too,
after the hospital. He's a deacon.

The woman and girl don't move.
The trolley doesn't move.
I hold my breath. It's very quiet.

I think, I'll be late to church. And,
This might be in the newspaper. Then,
sirens and the girl starts crying.

Next morning, there it is, on the front page:
two policemen have the woman by the arm.
The girl's not in the photo—where is she?

I'd like to be in the paper.
If it's something you can be proud of,
Father says. He asks if I behaved

myself, by which he means, Did I
say anything? I did not. That night,
in my notebook, I give the Negro girl

a name. Beatrice. Her slip showed,
I write. I give her a baby sister
and a father who is a deacon, too.

Impetigo

I knew not to tee-tee in the pool
(WHITES ONLY), a girl in angel wings
at the mother-daughter banquet.
I did it anyway, shameful
lazy me, because at nine

so little sin was mine. To tinkle
where I should not, then sit up straight
with the Baptists in a velvet pew,
the preacher forever railing
against *man's* nature, I had to.

Stand still. My brother and sisters lined up,
me, too, in the middle bedroom
to be painted in pink Mercurochrome.
The watery translucent blisters popped,
summer shimmered along, and I was falling

for the Catholic mysteries
of pretty Mrs. Brandon next door
who swore and smoked and held her beer.
She was forever *with child.*
Mary, must I be a mother?

Howie Oppenheimer, fourth grade,
hitch up your jeans. A girl not yet
marked as Christ's own forever
will soon sit two desks away. Get ready,
she's on to earthly pleasures.

Complicity

If you're under 15, you can't sit in the exit row.
Renting a car can't happen until you're 25,

but I could drive one in Louisiana at 16.
Hotel hot tubs also have age rules.

At five, I am reading, there's little else to do.
It isn't until high school, after students

from the Black school across town march,
that I ask, At what age am I responsible?

Negroes want better treatment. Every morning
it's in *The Shreveport Times* hitting our porch.

Girl Reporter, 1961

Billy Smithson, a football player from my school,
carries the cross and he holds it just so as he leads
the priests in white and gold down the wide aisle.

He doesn't see me. I'm in a back pew, my father
beside me, Christmas Eve at St. Mark's Episcopal.
Let's go, Daddy had said all of a sudden at bedtime

as if we'd already been talking about it, as if
he'd known I wanted to see inside the stone walls
I bike up to, only four blocks from our house.

Everyone but us knows what to do—when to kneel,
when to stand, the tune of the hymns, what page
in *The Book of Common Prayer*. I hear

words like "acknowledge" and "bewail," pleas
for mercy, *kyrie eleison*. I love it, but worry:
this is church but is it really church if the sermon

doesn't make you feel bad, and you'd better change?
Father's smitten, too, I can tell. But we won't be back,
this is for only one night. Too rich for us.

When we get home, everyone's asleep, no one
to tell about the lit candles and how incense
smells like being inside our clubhouse in the backyard,

like wood and earth but on fire. What does a cross
on fire smell like? One was thrown, I heard,
into the yard of a white couple friendly to Negroes.

The Absence of Romance in My History

We pulled down the shades and stayed inside
the day JFK was shot,
our lowered yellowing blinders my father's fear,
They'll riot now that their buddy's gone.
That bastard LBJ's in bed with them, too.

On nearby Dallas our kind TV-dined
on potted meat and powdered milk.
We were used to living lean—
surviving children of a defeated South.
How long could we hole up?

One day, that's all, one "O Say"
at the end of the TV viewing day,
Daddy talking talking talking
the skulking night away and then
we kids burst out, into the grievous streets.

Our Charity, 1963

They're coming to the high school!
Our high school. One at least.
No child of mine, my father begins,
and we know the rest. He's beside himself:

I'll yank you out of there, that's what I'll do.
Where will we go? St. Vincent's?
With rosaries, uniforms. Mass, incense?
I've been to a Catholic church exactly once.

We'll be in the news! Then, as the months pass
and the school board again delays,
it gets boring, Daddy going on and on,
he can't stop himself, best that we keep quiet.

We can't afford Catholic high school.
We can barely afford Centenary College
and that's where we'll go, my brothers
and sisters, too, just like our parents.

I try to picture the Negro boy.
I'll be nice. I'll say *Good morning*
when we pass in the hall. How kind I am,
how Christian. I might sit with him

at lunch once or twice. He'll be grateful.
The boyfriend who just dumped me
jealous. Oh! What if the new student
is a girl and doesn't even speak to me?

She might be mad as hell, like those kids
at Booker T. Washington across town.
They wanted to honor the little girls
killed by that bomb in Birmingham

and left school to march. Shreveport police
fired tear gas and drove them back
to Booker T, where ninth graders on up,
hundreds of them, cheered them on.

The Slattery Building

A building my father was proud to walk into,
proud to put on his business card, mention
to fellow deacons, and always a friendly word
to the Negro running the ornate elevator,

the Slattery Building, late Gothic,
was the tallest privately owned building
in the state when it was finished in 1924,
17 stories. The courthouse is across the street.

Leather chairs and drapes for the top floors.
My father's office mid-building had a metal desk,
a swivel chair, an oak bookcase, a filing cabinet, and
a coat rack on which he hung his brown felt hat.

His job was convincing officials to lower taxes
for Arkansas Louisiana Gas Co. A lawyer,
night school, no shame in that, and Slattery
wasn't the timber mill of his father.

Sometimes, my father checked out a company car
to argue taxes in Dallas. Elysian Fields. Gladewater.
He'd stay at a hotel good enough to supply a finger bowl
at dinner, which he insisted a gentleman required.

In the 60s, a Mr. Thomas was promoted over him.
By then, cigarettes/insomnia/bacon or sausage
every morning/and snarling at my mother had
Daddy mostly in the hospital. His heart.

He thought the company and his family ungrateful.
My father insisted on gratefulness. It makes it harder
now to enjoy him striding down Marshall Street to
a fine building. It's Christmas. He's bought presents

from Woolworth for the children. Should he tip
the soft-spoken man who runs the elevator?
He always knows his floor, always calls him
by name, *Mr. Victory*. How much would be right?

Diary, 1965

This family named Lemon is all the new boy at school talks about. The Lemons are at Barksdale, Air Force like his family, and they're suing Bossier Parish to desegregate the schools. This boy, Doug, admires them. The whole base does, he brags. Now, the kids, like other Negroes, have to go to Butler and Mitchell.

The Lemons' case is in the paper a lot. My father gets riled up, I warned Doug. *If you come to my house, not a word.* He says, *Come to my house again, we'll go to the pool at the base. The Lemon kids are there all the time.* Swimming with coloreds, what if Daddy found out?

I'd like to see Negroes who stand up for themselves. Is that military? Living outside Louisiana? Both? Doug's family lived on a base in Germany. He tells his mother she's *broad across the beam.* And his father just laughs. Do the Lemon kids talk to their mother like that?

Where He Started. Where He Got To.

On the school board, Ben Dawkins, Jr.
pushed for new schools for Negro children.
Educate our Negroes, he told the Rotarians,
eliminate slums, give them health care

and *economic opportunities*
commensurate with their abilities.
But integrate? It would lead to *mongrelization*
of both races, he said in the 1950 speech.

Three years later, Dawkins was a federal judge.
He began to approve delay after delay
to integrate the schools. Foot-dragging,
one historian called it.

Others called it gradualism.
Finally, a higher court told Shreveport
to end its dual school system at once.
That was 1969. Foot-dragging indeed.

Then in 1976, it was Dawkins who ruled
elections in Shreveport violated
minority voting rights. Blacks were soon
represented closer to their numbers.

...the arc of the moral universe is long
but it bends toward justice. As a child
in Monroe, Louisiana, Dawkins saw
a young Black man hanged and burned

by a mob on the courthouse square.
It didn't seem to make him more humane,
until it did. Dawkins could have been
one of my people—gradualists: today

no one in my family uses racist names.
I no longer hear the nursery rhyme
eeny meeny miny moe with a racist slur
substituted in *catch a tiger by the toe.*

Thanksgiving Over the Water

For the Red River flowing alongside Shreveport, water for cotton and rice, water to inject deep into the earth to bring up oil and natural gas.

For Henry Miller Shreve, born in New Jersey, who designed the "snag boat" that in 1839 cleared the river, so clogged with trees that a 150-mile stretch in North Louisiana was called The Great Raft.

For current that flowed after crews cleared the river of trees again and again, opening my town to shipping, to growth, to schooling that brought my father from Timpson, Texas, and my mother from tiny Oakdale, Louisiana, to the promise of Shreveport.

For the baptismal water at First Baptist Shreveport, when age 12, white-robed, I entered the thigh-deep water high above the altar, the pastor's face pouring sweat, his handkerchief gently pressed against my nose as he tilted me backwards, full immersion. Marked as Christ's own forever.

For the Sea of Galilee on which Jesus walked, pictured in the Bible I received at baptism.

For Cross Lake, formed by The Great Raft logjam. A church friend's father owned a boat. His patience as I tried to learn to water ski.

For my mother's hand wringer washer. Clothes for seven children to wash and hang on the line.

For water to fill the bathtub over and over Saturday night so my twin sister Ellen and I and our sisters and brothers would be clean for church.

For watermelon my father brought home from business trips in East Texas and we ate on the back porch.

For water from the hose to drench sweetpeas that grew on the side fence of our backyard, the cuttings taken from my great-grandmother's farm south of town.

For the waterbugs that brought out the warrior in my oldest brother, Steve, dead now 38 years. He squashed them in the bathroom, the kitchen, wherever they skittered. His vigilance on our behalf.

land of cotton, old times there are not forgotten

you'll never know how much—

look away, look away

The Whites Eat Lunch

How unaware she was growing up
of how Blacks in their hometown were treated,
Shame tells her twin Confession.

Not paying attention, that's a form of racism,
Shame says, and how unaware were they really?

Confession is used to this. As teenagers
Shame and Confession walked their neighborhood
Sunday afternoon and talked about their failures

and boys. They tried to comfort each other.
There was no one else to comfort them.

We didn't talk enough about race, Shame says.
Confession nods then sighs.

Here comes that Sunday feeling:
no resolution and no way to make it better.
We couldn't name a single Black person then,

Confession says. Shame suspects another sin,
wonders not for the first time if she can bear it.

Christian in Name

Mary the teenager visited by an angel,
Mary the believer who mourned at the tomb,
and *Mary* I was baptized

but what did Mary have to do with me?
It wasn't Mary who loved the little children
red and yellow and black and white,

it was Jesus on the Sunday School wall.
I never imagined a halo for myself.
Besides, I was called by my middle name,

Frances. My mother's brother Francis
was a Baptist minister in Mississippi, who,
according to some in the family, bragged

he'd stand at the church door to keep out
those people, if it came to that. What did
he think *those people* would do? No one said.

Our people, baptized as Christ's own forever,
believed. *Those people* did. When even at church
things get tense, what's Mary got to do with it?

Thirteen

I didn't thank God, I didn't curse God,
God didn't enter into it when suddenly
from my own body all this blood.

I was at my grandmother's and woke
to a soaked bed. My aunt found me crying
at the shame of it. She helped me clean up,

my aunt with no children of her own, and
was it then that she drew away from me,
threw herself into teaching my brothers tennis?

At church all was the same: shame, suffering,
the old rugged cross. But everything could change
just like that. It seemed faith didn't trump all

and not for my careful mother either—
her seven children to say grace over—who
in time got a doctor to give me birth control pills.

Mother's Lipstick

spreads rose by antique rose
through my garden
to her doilied vanity

where she sits in a white slip
painting Midnight Red peaks
over her lips' broad valley.

Then she's downtown to First Baptist
where He walks with her
and He talks with her

and He tells her she is His own.
Sustained, she comes home
full of *the joy we share*

and to newborn kittens—
that cat!—under the kitchen table
and not to be sung away.

Instead of a Rally for Justice

You have loved righteousness and hated wickedness;
therefore God, your God, has anointed you
with the oil of gladness…
—Hebrews 1:9

Just because the red-haired bully next door
moved to Fayetteville and you could skate
freely down the sidewalk again

and just because death moving
through the brain one lobe at a time
was arresting in *National Geographic,*

its path less terrifying in color,
doesn't mean the *oil of gladness*
would be a term applied to you

if loving righteousness and hating
wickedness are the standard. One bow
to the cross, that's enough, no extremes,

unlike your great-grandmother
who wrote your mother in 1943
…God is punishing the world now

for its greatest sin, desecration of His day….
by which she seemed to imply that God
caused WWII because people went visiting

on Sunday. You do keep the Lord's Day
but often, instead of a rally for justice,
you choose an afternoon of trying on shoes,

all that possibility, then return home
to lovingly wash the sheets
and make for yourself a fresh bed.

Lent

Fear of the other,
even the family next door,
was our sure defense.

They ate fish on Friday,
JFK was their man
and the pope his man.

The Brandons ignored
our ignorance, invited us over
to watch *American Bandstand,*

confident teens worlds away
dancing and singing.
Hallelujah, Lent or no. Lord,

give me something cleansing
for when I was a child,
a snagboat to break up

the logjam of inherited fear
when Lent meant *Catholic*
and was therefore suspicious.

Seven Years Before My Mother's Mother Dies

Grandmother keeps an eye out:
What's that fellow doing?

as if a man walking alone
after supper is itself suspicious.

Morning, she watches the street
from her bed. She dozes and watches.

Late afternoon, she surveys
from the screened porch, rocking.

I sit across from her in the glider.
What's that fellow doing? hangs

between us. What can we, a 14-year-old
and the only grandparent she has known,

her 86-year-old grandmother,
say to each other? The street—Dalzell—

honored an Episcopal priest who warned
Shreveport residents in 1873 about yellow fever,

telling them to flee. He nursed those who stayed,
three-quarters of whom became infected.

Some The Rt. Rev. Dalzell likely didn't know from Adam.
It was Jesus we worried we wouldn't recognize.

Atlantic City, N.J., 1964

At the Southern Baptist Convention, the motion
commended *open door* churches
and those that supported legal rights

for *black people*. It seemed to urge
fellow Baptists *through legislation and love*
to work toward the defeat of racism. It failed.

A substitute was quickly drawn up.
My own pastor presented it. Racial problems,
it said, had to be solved at the *local level*

and the word "autonomy" played a role.
That motion passed. No Baptist tells another
Baptist what to do or what a church should do.

Thirty years later, the convention apologized
for its *racism...whether consciously or unconsciously*.
But when it mattered most, my church

voted for self-rule, against a united public stand.
At sixteen, I already wasn't going to church much
and nobody tried to make me.

Resolve

—to a dress shop clerk

"My husband doesn't feel strongly
since the other fellow's Catholic
and distributes beer, for heavens' sake,
and my best friend says she's leaning
that way—the man *is* a Baptist—
and *The Shreveport Times* won't endorse,
it says, as both men are good Democrats
so I may just possibly consider
considering voting for the Negro."

Diary, 1966

She says *ain't*, she carries cigarettes in her fake leather purse and doesn't care if anyone sees. Her hair has got to be bleached and she's always chewing on a strand, it's gross. When she chews gum, she smacks. She's always with that boy with a motorcycle and they kiss right in the parking lot. She wears a red bra, I saw her getting dressed in Gym. She's stacked. I don't think she goes to church or at least not to our church or to the Methodists downtown where that new boy, Doug, goes. Her father wears a work shirt with stitching on the back. His car needs a new muffler. Her brother enlisted right out of high school. She never raises her hand and it's only Algebra I. She didn't even try out for Pep Squad. In English, she asks to go to the Girls' almost every day. When she cries—and she does at the drop of a hat—her nose doesn't get red, like mine.

Figs, Formica

I didn't bring figs for lunch
though plenty grew every year
behind the modest frame house

my father and grandfather had built.
Whether the figs were female or male
did not once occur to me

and eating a fig in one bite
I did not think vulgar.
I had not read Lawrence

so a fig was just a fig
and my house was just a house,
though not at all like my friend's.

My friend's father traded in his car
every three years. The Formica counters
in the kitchen must not be marred:

nothing hot should be set down.
If I had not been writing stories
for the school paper about girls

doing service projects and girls
going to summer camp, Formica
might have been used as a metaphor

for the tension inside houses,
including my own, and inside me,
and not always only about money.

The Presence of Romance in My History

It wasn't a word we said to each other—*romance*—
but through death we lived it. Christ's tragic end,

and that He did it for *us*, was a daily presence.
We'd meet again in Heaven. Still, the drama.

Men we knew died—Mr. Spence in middle school
leaving football-playing sons and a popular daughter.

Sunny Tommy from college killed himself. The brother
of a high school friend, too. *Our boys*, we were reminded,

died in the Civil War, which made it seem our tragedy.
They could have been brothers and boyfriends

and wasn't it a shame the cocky "Dixie" we sang
was no match for "The Battle Hymn of the Republic"?

Eartha Kitt

What we hear is not only sound,
it's memory—LBJ's twang,
my father's curled lip *N*—

What did Lady Bird silently
label her guest? Imagine, Ms. Kitt
arriving at the White House lunch

with other ladies to discuss youth violence
and she lashes out about Vietnam,
about young men so alienated

"they rebel in the streets."
Lady Bird's voice trembled and tears
welled up, not from sympathy.

Within weeks, most of Kitt's appearances
were cancelled. Her acting career floundered.
Years later she learned the president

had ordered the CIA to investigate her.
Don't you dare make Bird cry like that,
don't you dare criticize her husband's war,

not when the first lady was in Harlem
planting trees, and wildflowers would soon
come up all along the highways of America.

Lost

when he ran for school board, 1954,
the first Negro to run for public office
in Louisiana since Civil War days.

He lost a home being built in 1962
on Delores Street. Bombed.
The Southern Christian Leadership Conference

board member had already lost
his lawn at 1508 Gary Street
when a cross was burned there.

In 1990, he ran for mayor and lost
badly, though prominent whites supported him
and Blacks were by then 44 percent of the city.

When, finally in 1992, the activist dentist won,
it was to serve in the legislature. His successor
became Shreveport's first Black mayor.

*

You are not in this struggle alone,
Martin Luther King said in Shreveport
that night in August 1958, reassuring

himself and his listeners. Dr. C. O. Simpkins,
championing the rights of Blacks in
the most repressive of Louisiana cities

was there and the words were likely a comfort.
He'd have to wait years to hear that from others.
A street in Shreveport was named for him, in 2014.

The Whites at the Hardware

Shame and Confession are looking at a crèche
on sale post-Christmas at the hardware
when a woman they know walks up and during their chat
tells them that 40 years ago
she was named sweetheart of the basketball team
at her West Texas high school. Her mother
wasn't *particularly pleased,* she laughingly whispers,
because the team was mostly Black.
In this crèche, the wise men are in draped robes
with gold edging. The scene's so mannered,
the slightly bowing gift-givers, the composed Mary,
it could be a French play. Moliere.
One of Baby Jesus' arms is missing,
which is why the crèche is on the discount rack.
Some day, Shame tells Confession,
she wants to live among people wiser than her,
who would notice sooner than
a week after bringing the figures home
that Jesus of the hardware is white,
the men who come to pay homage, too,
and know right off, *Something's not right,*
as her computer screen has said all day
when she tried to get on. Such wise people
would not smile, as she did, when a woman she knows
whispers what *our people* used to think.

Bridge

Lead Belly's blues, born in Shreveport,
any music can be a bridge: *Amazing Grace;*
Goodnight, Irene; Tutti Frutti.
Blacks surely sang those. Whites did.

Whites read the Bible. Blacks read the Bible.
Whites fried chicken and ate cornbread.
Blacks fried chicken and ate cornbread.
School, church—hell—even sticky summer

could have been a bridge, except
Blacks swam in their neighborhood pools,
whites in theirs. At the movies,
did Blacks sit in the balcony? I never looked.

[My journey with grief well underway,
Shame taps me on the shoulder
to ask why I'm still at the river. I say,
The Red's my river. Confession: Still?]

Resolve

—to her sister

"Sallie Lou, guess what? Van Cliburn
may play a concert here! And—
you'll never guess—at First Baptist!
It was in the paper this morning.
He's just gotten back from Russia.
There's a picture of him with Khrushchev!
I think we ought to put up a statue of him,
he was born here, like the one outside the courthouse
of those Confederate generals. Well, maybe not so big."

Another City. Another Time. The Same.

Let our conversation be house
and driveway. Let us speak of wood
stirring spoons and the health of the car,
the hard-to-open front door, and Johnson
grass coming up again in driveway cracks.
Let us talk less and less of foundations.
Dvorak is playing in the house—
one of the Slavonic dances—for my brother
Steve who wanted (but did not get) music from *Cats*
at his funeral. My mother-in-law, taken the same year,
hums "Some Enchanted Evening."

It's Thanksgiving, a new president
has been elected. We must now speak of houses—
brick, ranch, for sale or lost, especially those lost—
as we would speak of many other necessaries,
in detail. A clamshell, quite like ones crushed
for the driveway, sits on a tiny shelf just inside
the house. Let this not be our main emblem
for all that one must build and protect.

Let us speak also of Kay next door,
who yelled across the drive at Ramon cutting the grass,
she'd report him. He looked near tears.
Lady, I was born here. The same neighbor
later shouted she loved when our family
stood in the backyard, thirty of us, and sang
"America the Beautiful."

When the Bishop Preached at the Royal Wedding, 2018

True, slavery was mentioned but only to testify
to the power of love, how even in captivity
slaves sang *There is a balm in Gilead /*
to make the wounded whole, the spiritual

Mrs. Dooley sang as she played the zither
Sunday night at First Baptist Shreveport.
It was lovely and soothing and no one
need be sad: slavery was over.

So was the time when slaves worshipped
alongside masters. At First Baptist, Richmond,
by 1836, more than three-quarters
of the 2400 members were Negroes.

But *their peculiar habits, views, and prejudices*
drew complaints. The Negroes, too, complained:
white members did not respect their ways of worship.
Eventually, the whites helped the slaves

and the few freedmen build their own church.
Then no whites had to sit beside hand-waving
and laughing and shouting like the bishop
at the wedding at Windsor. He went on too long,

some thought, the way a man does when full
of good news, the way a Black believer
shows his faith. It's not for everyone,
having to keep a straight face, as if in respect.

The Whites Visit Shreveport

Shrimp, then Southern Maid donuts,
drive past the frame house sold long ago,
the drugstore where they bought cigarettes
for their father, KOOLs. The arboretum
of native trees at their college. How lucky
for them it existed and gave scholarships.

Shame and Confession are home
for a family funeral, birthday, wedding,
returning niece. Talk is easy: church, schools,
houses, gardens, a new job, a tornado, a Benz
bought at a bargain, more church. Illness.
No one suggests they *get into* their past.

The city has another Black mayor,
a Democrat, once their family's party.
Shame and Confession sense the change
in power may be unwelcome, but keep quiet.
They don't want to *start something*. How bright
the children are, they say. They *are* bright.

Later, Shame, exhausting Shame, says,
What could we have done? She means,
about the injustice they saw growing up.
Confession, patient Confession, says,
Let's sing, and begins *Lift Every Voice and Sing*.
They know it from church, on MLK's birthday.

Shame would like to *get into it*: did
they fail to do what they should have?
God of our weary years
God of our silent tears
She finally rolls down her car window
and they belt it out, top of their voices.

Thanksgiving Over the Water

For the Southern Baptist Convention which, after many pitchers of ice water, in 1954 passed a statement supporting *Brown v. Board of Education.* It called the ruling consistent with the constitutional guarantee of equal freedom to all citizens and "the Christian principles of equal justice and love for all men."

For water in toilets Black women could use when shopping, thanks to the Black women in Shreveport who organized the Committee on Stores and to the merchants who gave in to the demands in 1955.

For the spit of grown women "cheerleaders" who yelled obscenities at the few white parents who walked their children into newly integrated schools in New Orleans in 1960, for television that showed white women could spit their racism as well as anyone.

For water in the home of two elderly Black women in East Feliciana Parish. They offered students from up North a place to stay and a bathroom to clean up in as they registered voters.

For the waters of the Mississippi flowing to New Orleans where lawyer A.P. Tureaud (surely baptized as an infant, good Catholic that he was) fought for justice in court. Tureaud was considered the dean of civil rights lawyers in Louisiana for almost 50 years.

For water the maid might have been running for laundry when the mother of Federal District Judge J. Skelly Wright told her: her son had ruled segregated public transportation in New Orleans was unconstitutional. The maid told Tureaud.

For water that put out the fire when a cross was burned on Judge Wright's lawn the night the Supreme Court upheld his ruling, May 31, 1958.

For water used daily in the office of Shreveport dentist Dr. C.O. Simpkins, baptism unknown, who helped found the Southern Christian Leadership Conference and was a friend of Martin Luther King, Jr.

For water to put out the fire suspiciously started at the summer cottage owned by Simpkins whose house was bombed, too, in 1961.

For ice water drunk during the 111 days picketers in Tallulah, La. protested, mid-60s, until the A&P grocery agreed to hire Blacks.

For water in which U. S. Supreme Court Justice Thurgood Marshall, Episcopalian, was likely baptized as an infant. He was not from Louisiana, but Louisiana and the nation were changed because of him.

For Querbes swimming pool in Shreveport where as children we went almost every afternoon in the summer. It was closed by city officials along with other city pools, if memory is correct, when forced to integrate.

For the Southern Baptist Convention, its leaders perhaps with iced tea at hand this time, which in 1995 apologized to African Americans for how hollow its 1954 resolution had been. It acknowledged the role slavery played in founding the SBC as well as indifference and opposition to civil rights on the part of white Southern Baptists. It also apologized for condoning and/or perpetuating individual and systemic racism.

For "Wade in the Water," the spiritual sometimes sung as a secret message to escaping slaves: Fast! Get into a creek or river, the pursuers are coming with their dogs.

Did water fountains in Shreveport still have signs *Whites Only* by the time I could read?

Notes

"Part I Epigraph." The last line of the epigraph borrows from the opening line of the first official Louisiana state song, adopted in 1932 and written by Vashti R. Stopher. I sang "Song of Louisiana" daily in my elementary school.

"Resolve." The full name of the group referred to is The Association of Southern Women for the Prevention of Lynching. It was begun in Atlanta in 1930 by Texas-born Jessie Daniel Ames. At its height, there were 109 affiliated chapters and four million members. It ended in 1942.

"Going Home. Who Comes With Me." I owe the image of a dog as grief to the poem "Talking to Grief" by Denise Levertov.

"For Alexander, Amos, Charlotte, Dicke, Durnbonell, George, Jacob, Jennie, Sarah, and Stephen." I rely here on a database of slaves owned by Matagorda County plantation owners. The introduction to the list provides the number of whites and the number of slaves living in the county in 1850 (see The USGenWeb Project).

Information on one of the probable owners, Cpt. John Rugeley, can be found online in *The Texas State Handbook.*

For information on John Rugeley's will and the newspaper ad he placed, I rely on a privately printed book by Arda Talbot Allen, *Twenty-One Sons for Texas.*

For information on the Shreveport slave market, I consulted the World Port Source's content on the port of Shreveport/Bossier.

Thomas S. Kidd and Barry Hankins' *Baptists in America, A History* describes Baptist assemblies opposed to slavery in the 1790s.

Rugeleys in America, Vol. II, compiled by Helen Rugeley and published privately by the Rugeley Family Association, describes on page 38 letters written by Henry to his brother Matthew, asking for money to buy Negroes.

"Resolve." I base the woman's thoughts on: "'Only new-comers in Alexandria say Miss, Mr., or Mrs. when addressing or speaking of Negroes,' stated W.J. Avery, the school superintendent of Rapides Parish," in a 1932 letter (see Adam Fairclough, *Race & Democracy, The Civil Rights Struggle in Louisiana, 1915–1972*). My poem suggests that would be true also in Shreveport, about two hours north.

"It Wasn't Us." I rely on the Equal Justice Initiative in Montgomery, Alabama, for the number of lynchings in Caddo Parish and how Caddo ranked with other parishes and counties in the country.

"Gladstone Boulevard." I am referring in part to Gladstone's speech at Newcastle-on-Tyne October 7, 1862, in which he supported Confederate independence, saying that Jefferson Davis "had made a nation." Gladstone later regretted the speech.

About a third of Sir John Gladstone's fortune was from investments in estates worked by slave labor, in Demerara in the West Indies (see Richard Shannon, *Gladstone 1809–65*).

"Resolve." A funeral is planned for a body returned after being buried in an Italian cemetery. Beginning in 1947, the government offered to pay to have the remains of soldiers shipped back to the United States from foreign burial sites. A large number of families took advantage of the offer.

"When Martin Luther King, Jr. Spoke in Shreveport, 1958." The references to police action on the night of August 14 are made by Shreveport civil rights activist Dr. C. O. Simpkins. All the other references in the poem are from the speech itself.

"Resolve." Elvis Presley performed on the *Louisiana Hayride* 1954–56; the show was broadcast from a 50,000-watt KWKH radio in Shreveport.

"Girl Reporter, 1961." The cross was burned in the yard of Ethel and Joe Daniell of Shreveport.

"Our Charity, 1963" was inspired by Beryl Jones, Arthur Burton, and Brenda Braggs who enrolled in my high school, C. E. Byrd, in 1965. They were the first Blacks to attend a previously all-white school in Caddo Parish (see Provizer, Norman W. and Pederson, William D., *Grassroots Constitutionalism: Shreveport, the South, and the Supreme Law of the Land*).

"Diary, 1965." See *G. I. Joe v. Jim Crow: Legal Battles Over Off-Base School Segregation of Military Children in the American South, 1962–64*, a 2016 dissertation by Randall George Owens. Ben Dawkins, Jr. was the federal judge in the case.

For more on the legacy of Dawkins, see *Grassroots Constitutionalism*. The italicized lines near the end of "Where He Started. Where He Got To." are from a speech Martin Luther King gave March 31, 1968, at the National Cathedral in Washington, DC.

"Part II Epigraph." The first and last line borrow from "Dixie," written by Daniel D. Emmett and published in 1859. The middle line is from one of Louisiana's many official state songs, "You Are My Sunshine." It was written by Jimmie Davis and Charles Mitchell and recorded in 1939.

"Christian in Name." I am referring to the song "Jesus Loves the Little Children."

"Mother's Lipstick." I am paraphrasing lines from the hymn "In the Garden."

"Lost." Dr. Simpkins ran for school board in either 1952 or 1954; interviews and other sources offer conflicting information. The statement that he was the first Negro to run for office in Louisiana since the Civil War is from an article by Mary McCrory in *The Atlanta Constitution*. McCrory's statement does not define "run for office" or "Civil War days." P. B. S. Pinchback, an African American, stepped in as lieutenant governor to serve as interim governor of Louisiana after the impeachment of Gov. Henry C. Warmouth. Pinchback served from December 9, 1872, to January 13, 1873, or 35 days. He was the only Black governor of any state during Reconstruction.

"In 1961 and 1962, the Klan dynamited a black Masonic lodge, threw firebombs at a church during a CORE [Congress of Racial Equality] meeting, blew up a new home being built for Dr. Simpkins, and set fire to Simpkins' summer cottage." (Fairclough)

The Southern Christian Leadership Conference was formed in 1957; Simpkins was one of its founding members and served as its vice president when Martin Luther King was president.

Fairclough refers to Shreveport as "long the most repressive of Louisiana cities."

"Bridge." Lead Belly was born Huddie William Ledbetter at the Jeter Plantation near Mooringsport, Louisiana, about 1885. He often wrote his name as one word—Leadbelly. My mother sang one of his songs, "Goodnight, Irene," washing dishes.

"Resolve." Van Cliburn won the first International Tchaikovsky Competition in Moscow in 1958. He was born in Shreveport in 1934; his family lived there until he was six.

The memorial that sat in front of the Caddo Parish Courthouse was removed in 2022 after a five-year legal battle. It was erected in 1906 and had busts of Generals Lee, Jackson, Beauregard and Brigadier General Henry Allen, later Governor of Louisiana, 1864–65.

"When the Bishop Preached at the Royal Wedding, 2018" describes the homily given at the May 19, 2018 wedding of England's Prince Harry and American actress Meghan Markle at George's Chapel at Windsor

Castle. The Most Rev. Michael B. Curry, the presiding bishop of the Episcopal Church, refers to the spiritual, "There Is a Balm in Gilead."

First Baptist Church in Richmond was founded in 1780. Slave members were prominent from the beginning and soon came to outnumber whites. Almost half of the members of the church my family attended, First Baptist Shreveport, were Black before, in 1866, those members formed their own church, Antioch Baptist.

"Thanksgiving Over the Water."

[SBC, 1954 decision]: The Southern Baptist Convention often supported civil rights with official recommendations even while most Southern Baptists opposed integration. The 1954 meeting adopted a statement supporting the *Brown* decision, acknowledging that it was consistent with the constitutional guarantee of equal freedom to all citizens and "the Christian principles of equal justice and love for all men."

[For toilets]: The Committee also asked merchants for fitting rooms Black women could use.

[For cheerleaders]: A story in *The Times-Picayune* of New Orleans recounted by historian Adam Fairclough describes how the few white parents who kept their children in these schools "ran a gauntlet of between forty to two hundred [white] mothers, their faces contorted with rage, shrieking threats and obscenities."

[For two elderly Black women]: The two women were Josephine "Mama Jo" Holmes, age 74, and Charlotte Greenup, in her 80s. (Fairclough)

[For waters . . . Tureaud]: Alexander Pierre Tureaud (1899–1972) was a Creole and light-skinned. He might have been able to pass as white. He fought racial discrimination for half a century in Louisiana, often through the courts and, for a time, he was the only Black lawyer in the state. His law partner, Ernest N. Morial, became the first Black mayor of New Orleans, in 1977. His son, A. P. Tureaud, Jr. was Louisiana State University's first Black undergraduate. (Fairclough)

[For water to put out the cross burning on Judge Wright's lawn]. The decision about New Orleans busses was in 1957. Wright was the youngest federal judge (38) in the country and only one year on the bench when he wrote the opinion in 1950 that forced Louisiana State University to accept its first Black law student. He said, "Until that day I was just another Southern 'boy.' After that, there was no turning back." (Fairclough)

[For ice water]: In Madison Parish, a majority-Black parish, no Blacks voted before December 1962. The boycott of Tallulah businesses was started by the Madison Parish Voters League, a Black organization, because businesses were not hiring Black sales clerks. Seventeen businesses closed their doors rather than succumb to pressure.

[For "Wade in the Water"]: Harriet Tubman is described as singing the spiritual to alert escaping slaves to dogs.

[Did water fountains?]: One example of continuing discriminatory practices was airports. Lawsuits and "eat-ins" and various other methods forced airports to change, but there were holdouts. Finally, in 1961, the Department of Justice filed suits against the airports in Montgomery and New Orleans and then in 1962, against Shreveport and Birmingham. Using testimony, images, and floor plans, it proved that "the airport management and the restaurant proprietor systematically discriminated against black travelers by posting signs and segregating along racial lines the airport's waiting, eating, drinking, and restroom facilities." The court ruled in favor of the government. Shreveport appealed and lost and "the last signs at an American airport leading travelers to segregated facilities were ordered to come down on July 10, 1963 (see "The Desegregation of Airports in the American South" on the National Air and Space Museum website). I was 15.

Acknowledgments

Thank you to the following journals whose interest in a difficult subject kept me at my desk.

The Louisville Review	"Eartha Kitt"
Borderlands	"The Absence of Romance in My History"
Visions International	"Another City. Another Time. The Same" (originally published as "House and Driveway")

Writing a book of poems about my hometown has been humbling. How little I knew of Shreveport when living there. How little I still know of others' experience of the city.

Thank you, Casie Dodd of Belle Point, most thoughtful of editors. I am grateful with every email exchange. Jan Freeman, Joan Houlihan, and Nick Courtright saw the potential in *Whitewash* and helped tighten the book. Matt Knox has been a reader of my poems for years and should have been thanked in my first book. The steadfast writing group I am a part of improved these poems month by month.

My husband Pete is not from Shreveport. Lucky for me, though, his family values traits I learned from my own, the Victorys: hard work, loyalty, and support for each other. Readers every last one of them, too, lucky me.

Frances Victory Schenkkan is the author of *Mr. Stevens' Secretary* (University of Arkansas Press). A National Poetry Series finalist, Schenkkan has published in *The Southern Review*, *POOL*, *The Louisville Review*, and *Third Coast*, among others. She grew up in Shreveport and now lives in Austin.

Belle Point Press is a literary small press
along the Arkansas-Oklahoma border.
Our mission is simple: Stick around and read.
Learn more at **bellepointpress.com**.

www.ingramcontent.com/pod-product-compliance
Lightning Source LLC
LaVergne TN
LVHW051017080826
845145LV00009B/2672